CAN I BE THE (

FIVE SHORT PLAYS

PONT BOOKS

Contents

Twm was Here

Ruth Lee

Characters:

Rhodri:
Bethan:
Dad:
Mam: } The Morgan family, who run the Erwain hotel

Brad (son):
Mike (father): } The American family on holiday
Angie (mother):

SCENE 1 *Reception area of the hotel. Dad is bent over some papers scattered all over the counter. Mam is up a ladder, mending a fuse. Bethan is playing with a basketful of puppies while Rhodri sits on the stairs in his pyjamas, eating a bowlful of cornflakes.*

Bethan: Look, Mam! They're opening their eyes – see?

Dad: Your mother can't look, Bethan – she's up a ladder. Don't get too used to those pups, my girl. We'll be finding homes for them sooner rather than later.

Bethan: Aw, Dad. Can't we just keep one? The little smudgy one, he's my favourite.

Dad: No way: we haven't the money to keep them unless trade picks up. End of story.

Bethan: But *Dad!*

Dad: No means no, Bethan. Don't keep on! And Cally shouldn't be in here with her pups, anyway. It might put guests off, if that's the first thing they see as they walk through the door. It's not hygienic. Now I don't want any long faces: I want that basket out in the shed before I get back from town. (*Exit Dad*)

Bethan: Mam, why is Dad so snappy this morning?

Mam: He's doing the books, love. He's worried: we haven't had a single guest since last Thursday and it's the height of the season. If it carries on like this . . . well, Dad doesn't mean to take it out on you, bach.

Rhodri: Is it really serious, then?

Mam: Good heavens, no! Nothing for you to worry about. You could make yourselves useful, though. Bethan, tidy those leaflets, would you please? They're looking a bit of a mess. Rhodri, when you've quite finished your breakfast – which at this rate will be lunchtime – you can hoover the dining room. Right! I'll be out the back, painting. If the 'phone goes, you know what to say?

Bethan: *(best telephone voice)* Bore da. Erwain Hotel. How may I help you?

Mam: And give me a shout if it's someone wanting to book a room. (*Exit Mam*)

Bethan: Oh, you poor dabs! Fancy sticking you out in the shed!

Rhodri: Don't be silly, they'll be fine this time of year. Look, Beth, things are more serious than Mam is letting on.

Bethan: How do you mean?

Rhodri: I heard them talking late last night. Arguing, actually. It's getting so bad, with guests not turning up and everything, I even heard Dad say we should sell the hotel.

Bethan: Sell it? But we've always lived here!

Rhodri: That's what the argument was about.

Bethan: Stupid guests! Why aren't they turning up, then? I'd love to come here for a holiday – well, I wouldn't really, I'd sooner go to Florida like Shelley Phillips. We never go anywhere, stuck here all summer long . . .

Rhodri: Huh! That remark's a fat lot of help.

Bethan: What can we do then?

Rhodri: Don't know. Look at all these leaflets. It's a shame we're not right near any of these touristy places: *Roman Gold mines . . . Red Kite spotting . . .* we're too far from anywhere. People just seem to miss us.

Bethan: That red kite place, it's near the dam, isn't it? It was great when our class went up to the nature reserve. That's where Twm Sion Cati had his cave. Carys and I were pretending to be highwaymen: 'Stand and deliver: your money or your life!'

Rhodri: Pity we can't hold up a car full of tourists and say the same thing.

Bethan: Now who's being silly?

Rhodri: Well, Twm Sion Cati robbed from the rich to give to the poor. 'The Welsh Robin Hood' they call him.

Bethan: Do you think he ever galloped past our house?

Rhodri: Probably did at some point.

Bethan: Could you imagine if he actually stayed here? Stayed the night to avoid getting captured, slept in one of the rooms!

Rhodri: The visitors would come flocking, wouldn't they? . . . But, hang on a minute, who's to say he didn't?

Bethan: Huh?

Rhodri: Who's to say that Twm Sion Cati didn't stay here? Who can possibly prove he didn't?

Bethan: As long as the house was here, of course.

Rhodri: This house wasn't, but there was an older house on the same site. Burnt down or something, I heard Dad telling a guest. Both houses could have the same foundations.

Bethan: He could have slept the night in the cellar!

Rhodri: This is it, Beth: the perfect way to pull in the visitors and save our home! Mam and Dad mustn't get wind of it, though, they'd just put a stop to it.

Bethan: What are we going to do exactly?

Rhodri: Let's get these jobs done and we'll work it out upstairs. We're going to need the computer for this.

SCENE 2 *At the roadside, later that day. Bethan has been standing one side of the road, Rhodri the other. Bethan marches over to Rhodri.*

Bethan: This is pointless. Nobody's stopped. I'll give it five more minutes, then I'm off.

Rhodri: A couple of cars did slow down. Perhaps you should have made the signs bigger.

Bethan: I did my best. That was all the cardboard I could find. Maybe what you told me to write wasn't clear enough. (*Reads*) 'TWM SION CATI SLEPT HERE. STOP FOR DETAILS.' It doesn't say who he was or anything.

Rhodri: But when they stop we hit them with a leaflet telling them all that . . . Look, there's someone coming, smile at them!

Bethan: I don't believe it, they're slowing down.

Rhodri: They're stopping!

Bethan: I feel queasy.

The Fisher family is inside the car. The electric window slowly winds down. The Fishers all speak with an American accent.

Mike: Say, this Twm Sion Cati character. Is he the guy we've been hearing about, kind of 'The Welsh Robin-Hood'?

Rhodri: Yes, please take a free leaflet.

Bethan: Although many people think of Robin Hood as the English Twm Sion Cati!

Rhodri: (*whispering*) Sshh! There's no need to say that!

Angie: Oh, Brad, you remember, honey? We saw that talking statue back in the heritage place – it's the same guy.

Brad: (*bored*) Yeah, Mom, I remember.

Mike: It says here he spent the night at this hotel, escaping from the law.

Rhodri: Although it wasn't a hotel then, of course. It wasn't even the same house.

Brad: How come he slept in this house, if it wasn't the same house?

Rhodri: There was an older house, built on the same site as this one. Legend has it, he slept down the cellar.

Angie: Oh, how fascinating!

Brad: Yeah, sure.

Bethan: In fact, legend has it he got drunk that night and buried all the money he'd stolen somewhere in the cellar but when he woke up the next morning, he'd forgotten where he'd put it.

(Rhodri begins to cough loudly)

Mike: It doesn't say anything about that in the leaflet.

Brad: So the money's still there?

Bethan: Who knows? That's how the legend goes.

Angie: Oh, Mike, it's such a thrilling story! Let's stop the night. The kids are cute, too – they'd be company for Brad.

Mike: What do you say, Brad?

Brad: *(brightening)* Yeah, why not stop the night.

9

Mike: Okay, kids. You've sold us the idea. Just lead the way . . .

SCENE 3 *Hotel Reception area. Mam is behind the counter. The Fishers are checking in.*

Rhodri: *(whispering to Bethan)* Why did you have to say about him getting drunk and burying the money?

Bethan: *(to Rhodri)* It did the trick, didn't it? They weren't going to stop until I said that.

Rhodri: *(to Bethan)* Well, just stick to the story in future, or we'll be in deep trouble.

Mam: There, that's all the paperwork done, Mr and Mrs Fisher. My goodness, Chicago! You have come a long way.

Mike: Well, it was worth it. The countryside round here sure is beautiful.

Angie: And your history is so interesting. Rhodri and Bethan were just telling us about Twm Sion Cati.

Mam: Oh, yes, he was a very popular local figure. Thomas Jones was his real name.

Mike: Indeed? We're looking forward to finding out more about him.

Rhodri: *(cutting in)* Bethan and I can tell you all you need to know but first of all, shall we help you carry your bags upstairs?

Brad: Sure. And then we get to see the cellar, right?

Mam: Er, the cellar?

Brad: I'd really like to see it.

Bethan: *(in a whisper, to Mam)* He's never seen one before. They don't have them in America.

Mam: Oh, the cellar! Of course! Whatever you need to make your stay enjoyable. Bethan knows where the keys are kept.

Angie: Thank you so much. You have such adorable kids. I'm sure they'll be better than any guidebook!

SCENE 4 *Four days later. In the yard, Bethan has just put the pups back in the shed after playing with them. It is nearly lunchtime. Enter Rhodri.*

Rhodri: Guess what? They're staying another two days.

Bethan: How come? They were supposed to leave this morning.

Rhodri: They're in love with the place. Mr and Mrs Fisher are off in their car for the day again. They'll know the area better than we do by the time they've finished. Of course, Brad's still in bed.

Bethan: Well, Mam and Dad should be pleased.

Rhodri: They're only one family, Beth. That's hardly going to save us. And to tell you the truth, I don't know how much longer I can keep up this Twm Sion Cati thing. I keep thinking we're about to get found out.

Bethan: I know what you mean. I've been feeling a bit, well, guilty. They're a really nice family. At least Mr and Mrs Fisher haven't asked us anything about it for a few days.

Rhodri: No, but Brad does.

Bethan: All the time . . .

Rhodri: And look, Beth, I wish you'd stop adding more bits onto the legend. We said we'd stick to our original story.

Bethan: I can't help it, I just get carried away.

Rhodri: But carving 'TWM WAS HERE' on the wall of the cellar?

Bethan: *(giggling)* Your face when you saw that! Sshh! He's coming.

(Enter Brad, yawning. He has evidently just got up.)

Brad: Hi there. Where did my folks go?

Rhodri: Out for the day. They left you a note at reception.

Brad: I'd rather stay here, anyways. Is that okay with you guys?

Rhodri: Of course. We can do something. Get the old table tennis stuff out, maybe?

Brad: That sounds swell. *(Yawns)* A little later perhaps.

Bethan: Brad, do you always sleep in this late at home?

Brad: No, it must be your Welsh air.

Bethan: Oh.

Brad: Actually, I did have some difficulty getting to sleep last night. I was thinking about Twm Sion Cati . . .

Rhodri: It's just a legend, Brad. Forget about it.

Brad: Forget about it? Look, does the legend say how often he came back to look for the money he hid?

Bethan: He's never stopped looking.

Brad: Huh?

Bethan: *(in a warning voice)* It really is better if you forget about it, Brad. Especially as it's nearly full moon. They say every full moon, Twm returns to look for his money and he doesn't take kindly to people poking their noses into his business. So if you hear the pounding of hooves and neighing outside the window, don't look out, whatever you do!

Rhodri: *(to himself)* Give me strength!

SCENE 5 *Late that night. We are in the cellar in pitch darkness. Brad's shouts are heard, then many other voices and footsteps from above.*

Brad: Help! Help me someone!

Angie: Brad, honey, is that you?

Mike: Brad, where are you, son?

Brad: Here, down here. Help, it's trying to get me!

Dad: What's going on down there? Rhodri? Bethan?

Rhodri:
Bethan: } No, we're here.

Dad: Let me through quickly. I know where the light switch is.

The light comes on. Brad is lying on the floor of the cellar with a spade at his side. Scrambling to his feet, he backs away from something on the ground. The others descend the stairs.

Dad: What on earth has been going on?

Angie: *(rushing over to Brad)* Oh Mike, he's terrified! It's okay now, honey, Mom's here.

Brad: B – b – but look! There it is! I dug it up, I didn't mean to. I thought it was something to do with the ghost. Then the torch fell out of my hand and the light went out.

Mam: Ghost? What ghost is he talking about?

Angie: Urgh! It's hideous, it's some kind of skull!

The others move round the object and investigate it.

Mike: I wouldn't worry, son. There's nothing ghostly about this ol' guy. Belonged to a real live horse at one time. Ain't going nowhere, now.

Brad: A horse? Then that'll be *his* horse! The one you hear when there's a full moon.

Dad: Excuse me, can we have some kind of explanation for all this? Half the earth has been dug up down here.

Mike: I guess you owe these folks an apology, Brad. He'll pay for any damage, of course. I guess it was too much of a temptation for him, the thought of buried treasure lying around, unclaimed all these years.

Mam: Buried treaure?

Angie: Twm Sion Cati's treasure. The money he buried when he spent the night here.

Mam: I'm sorry, I haven't a clue what you're on about.

Angie: But you must do! The legend? The one Rhodri and Bethan told us, the reason we came to stay here in the first place?

Dad: Rhodri! Bethan! Explanations, this minute!

SCENE 6 *Three weeks later. Mam and Rhodri are in the kitchen, shelling peas. Bethan runs in with a letter.*

Bethan: It's a letter from Brad in the States!

Mam: Hmm. It's a wonder he wants anything to do with you two, the shock you let him in for.

15

Rhodri: It's not our fault he set up his own excavations down there. Digging away night after night with Dad's spade. No wonder he couldn't get up in the morning.

Bethan: And it's not as if we planted the skull for him to find. Pure luck, that was.

Mam: Well, I suppose we have done quite well out of it.

Bethan: 'MARI LWYD' UNEARTHED IN HOTEL CELLAR! The picture in *The Western Mail* was brilliant!

Mam: Well, that's what they *think* it could be. I didn't realise it was ever a custom round these parts, carrying a horse's head from house to house at New Year.

Rhodri: There were customs like that all over the place. The archaeologist said the skull was sometimes buried for the rest of the year. Just think: someone could have buried ours hundreds of years ago!

Mam: What does Brad have to say then, Bethan?

Bethan: He's missing Wales . . . told all his friends about the adventure . . . wants a photocopy of the article from the paper . . . and his parents send their love.

Mam: Such nice people, and so understanding.

Bethan: They did say it was the best holiday they'd ever had. We did them a favour, enticing them in!

Mam: Don't push it! Especially not in front of your father.

Dad enters humming, carrying the account books under his arm. He stops and they stare at him.

Bethan: Tell us, then! What did the accountant say?

Dad: He said we're not out of the woods yet, but if it carries on like this, it looks as if we'll be okay.

Rhodri, Bethan and Mam all cheer.

Mam: Well, the guests do seem to be finding us these days.

Rhodri: It's the publicity that's doing it.

Dad: Hmmm, you two! I still don't know whether to be cross with you or . . .

Bethan: Give us a medal?

Rhodri: Never mind that, we need to make sure the guests keep coming. We should display the Mari Lwyd somewhere prominent, like in the hallway and get some posters printed up, a new advert in the Yellow Pages, that sort of thing. Look, I was working on the computer this morning and I came up with an idea for a leaflet. No, Dad, don't look like that, it's the way it works these days . . .

Bethan: Believe us, Dad. It pays to advertise!

Whatever Happened to Fred?

Nicola Davies

Characters:

Teifion:
Tom:
Phil:
Dai: } pupils at Melin Arthur School
Zak:
Kim:

A man in a cloak (non-speaking)

Lunch-time at Melin Arthur Primary School; we can hear children's voices outside. Curtains open onto an empty classroom. In one corner is a large sign 'Melin Arthur School Pets' Corner'. Underneath the sign is a jar labelled STICK INSECTS, *a small cage labelled* HARVEY *and another,* FRED'S HOUSE

The door opens. Teifion, looking conspiratorial, comes in carrying a bunch of keys. He locks the door behind him and goes over to Pets' Corner. *He opens the door of* Fred's House *and searches around inside, looking miserable.*

He starts moving desks to the back of the room.

Someone knocks the door: three raps, silence, two raps. In reply, Teifion raps once. The person outside repeats the sequence.

Teifion: Who goes there?

Voice: Owain.

Teifion: Owain who?

Voice: Owain Glyndŵr. Let me in, Uncle Jasper.

Teifion unlocks the door to a small, skinny boy, real name Tom. He scans the corridor, ushers Tom into the room and locks the door. Tom rushes over to Fred's House *and peers in.*

Tom: He's not back.

Teifion: Of course he's not back. What are you looking in there for?

Tom: Sorry.

Teifion: Use your head in future. Think, mun! Well, don't just stand there. Give us a hand with the ring. Lord Rhys will be here any minute.

They move all but one desk to the back of the room, then place six chairs in a circle round the desk. Teifion clambers onto a chair, surveying the circle from above. Tom watches nervously.

Tom: What now, Teifion?

Teifion: (*crossly*) I'm Jasper. Call me Jasper.

Tom: Sorry, Ty . . . Sorry, Jasper. What shall I do now?

Teifion: Move that chair. That one there. No, not that one, the one next to it. To the right. That's your left. Right. The other way. That's it. Right.

Someone knocks on the door; an adult voice calls 'Anyone there?' The two boys freeze. After a few seconds, the teacher goes away.

Tom: They've gone.

Teifion: Sshh. Keep your voice down.

Three raps, silence, two raps. Teifion climbs down and goes to the door. He raps once. As before, the sequence is repeated.

Teifion: Who goes there?

Voice: Rhys.

Teifion: Rhys who?

Voice: Lord Rhys ap Thomas. Let me in, Uncle Jasper.

Teifion unlocks the door to Philip, a tall gloomy-looking boy who is into bullying anyone who appears weaker than him. He looks round the room critically, then nods his approval. He takes a baseball cap from his pocket and puts it on backwards, the peak facing behind him. Then he takes an eye-patch from the other pocket and arranges it over his left eye.

Teifion: Where's the book?

Philip: Colin's got it. It's his turn to look after it.

Teifion: Whew! I thought you must have lost it.

Tom: *(wailing)* What if you had?

Teifion: Well, he hasn't. Col's got it. *Dim panic. (To Philip, calmly)* Please be seated, Lord Rhys.

Philip climbs over the chairs, inspects them, brushes the dust off and sits down on the one he considers the cleanest.

Tom: Do *I* sit down now, Ty?

Teifion frowns at Tom

Tom: *(miserably)* Sorry. Jasper. I forgot.

Teifion: Well you'd better remember. And fast. It's Jasper, pizza face. And in case you've forgotten his name, too, that's not Phil, it's Lord Rhys.

Tom: Sorry, Ty . . . I mean Jasper. Please, Jasper, where do I sit?

Phil: You don't. Not yet, anyroad. Not till the others have sat down. And if you call me Phil in meetings, you'll be out on your . . .

Tom: Yes, Lord Rhys.

More knocks on the door, three raps, silence, two raps, silence. Teifion knocks once in reply.

Teifion: Who goes there?

Voices: The Stanley boys: Sir William Stanley and Lord Stanley. Let us in Uncle Jasper.

Teifion unlocks the door to two more boys, Dai and Zak

Teifion: Hurry up! Teachers about.

Dai: It's only Mrs Lemon. She's gone into the hall now.

Teifion: Right then. So get in here. Quick.

He locks the door after them.

Phil: *(In a hollow voice)* Take your seats, men. Come into the ring.

They all sit down, Tom waiting till everyone else is seated before he dares sit. They all look at the empty chair.

Phil: Col's late.

Zak: 'e's not coming.

Teifion: Course he is. I saw him in Maths and he gave me the eyeblink. He has to come. He's got the book

Tom: Col's not coming. What are we going to do?

Teifion: *(ignoring Tom and speaking to Phil)* Course he's coming.

Zak: He's not. Take his chair away, Owain,

Tom's forgotten he's Owain. He takes no notice.

Zak: Owain! Can't you even remember your own name?

Tom springs to life and picks up the spare chair.

Teifion: Put that chair back.

Tom: But . . .

Teifion: Colin will be here any minute.

Zak and Dai: No, he won't.

Phil: One of you, go and get him.

Dai: We can't. He's gone to chess club.

Teifion: He can't have. He's got the book.

Tom: *(wailing)* What are we going to do about Fred?

As they stare at each other helplessly, there are knocks on the door: the usual sequence.

Teifion: *(relieved)* That'll be Col now.

He raps on the door. The person outside repeats the sequence.

Teifion: Who goes there?

There is no answer. Teifion is baffled. He looks at Philip for guidance. Philip looks equally baffled. The knocks come again. Teifion raps once and the knocks repeat themselves.

Teifion: Who goes there?

Voice: (*gruff and deep*) Just let me in, Teifion Harry.

Tom: (*panicking*) Oh, no! It's the 'edmaster.

Phil: Can't be the 'ead. He don't know the knocks. Let Col in, Ty.

Teifion: OK. Just stop looking so scared, you lot. It'll be alright now Colin's here. We'll get Fred back.

Teifion unlocks the door slowly and opens it. As soon as he sees who it is, he slams it shut again and leans against it.

Zak: Who is it?

Teifion: It's Kimberly Beynon.

Dai: (*shocked*) Girls!

Kim: If you don't let me in, I'll tell the 'ead about you all.

The boys look at each other. Phil nods at Teifion, who reluctantly opens the door. Kimberly, carrier bag in hand, strides into the room and nods grimly at the group.

Kim: (*to Teifion*) Hadn't you better lock up? There's teachers about.

Teifion does so, still keeping his eyes on her.

Tom: How did you know the secret knocks?

Kim: That's not secret knocks . . . three, two, one. You might have come up with something a bit more original than that. That's the trouble with boys: no imagination. (*Coming up to Philip*) So. What's going on? Is this your version of King Arthur and the Knights of the Round Table? Long John Philip and the Frights of the Multiplication Table? Where's your parrot, boy?

Phil: Ha. Ha. Very funny. Naff off, Kimberly. We got private things to discuss.

Kim: I bet you have.

Dai: And what's that supposed to mean?

Kim: I know about you and Fred.

Dai: (*scared*) You do?

Phil: She doesn't know anything. Go away, Kimberly. We got important things to discuss.

Kim: About how to get Fred back, you mean? Look, I don't know what you done with him, but I do know you lot took him from his cage. Fred's my responsibility. I've brought him a lettuce. You've got to bring him back.

Teifion: That's what we're trying to do, bring him back. But we can't while you're here.

Kim: Don't be so daft. I'm not moving from here till you tell me where he is.

Tom: (*in despair*) That's just it. We don't know.

Phil: Shut up, you fool!

Kim: I'm surprised at you, Teifion. I thought you had better things to do than kidnap tortoises.

Teifion: Kidnap? We haven't kidnapped Fred.

Kim: Oh no? Then where is he? What have you done with him?

Tom: (*wailing*) We didn't *do* anything. He just disappeared.

The boys try to shut TOM up.

Kim: I'll give you two minutes to tell me what you've done with him, or I'm off to see the head about cruelty to animals.

The boys look to each other for rescue. Then, Phil's eyes light up.

Phil: Shall we send you where Fred is?

Dai and Zak are delighted, but Teifion and Tom shake their heads.

Teifion: You can't do it, Phil. Anyway, we can't send her off without the book.

Kim: The book? You mean this old thing? (*She fishes a battered old green book out of her carrier bag*) Don't look so surprised. I nicked it out of Col's locker after I saw him hiding it there. He's been going spare all morning, looking for it.

Teifion: That must be why he's not here. Afraid we'll duff him up for losing it.

Kim: *(looking through the pages)* What's so special about this, then? It's just an old history book. *(She reads aloud)* 'The greatest was the revolt of Owain Glyndŵr in the first dec ... the first decade of the fifteenth century ...'

Before she can continue, Teifion rushes over to her, and puts his hand over her mouth.

Teifion: *(scared)* Stop! Close the book! Stop reading!

Kimberly is so taken aback, she shuts the book. The boys are so frightened that it scares her, too.

Kim: What is it?

Teifion: That book. It's haunted.

Kim: Teifion, mun. You've gone doolally.

Dai: It's true. That book ... it made Fred disappear.

Kim: You what?

She looks at their worried faces, then sits down in the empty chair and speaks to Teifion.

Kim: You mean it, don't you? About Fred.

Teifion: He just disappeared.

Kim: So Colin was telling the truth.

Dai: He told you? But he promised ...

Kim: I know all about your secret society. It's not Col's fault. He asked me out, and I said I wouldn't if he didn't tell me where he got to Tuesday lunchtimes.

Zak: But the rules.

Kim: I know: 'Tell no-one, even if they torture you.' Well, I did torture him and he told me all about your silly meetings. All about the knocks and Phil bossing everyone around and wearing that stupid eyepatch and how everyone has a daft name, and you do chanting . . . and then the bell goes and you go to lessons. What's that got to do with Fred vanishing?

Teifion: Watch this.

Phil: No, Ty!

Teifion: It's the quickest way. Sit down, everyone. You too, Kim.

He goes to the back of the room and comes back with a chair. He stands it on the desk. Then he takes a small torch from his pocket and hands it to Kimberly.

Teifion: When I say 'ON' switch it on.

Kim: Right-ee-o.

He takes the book from her hand, opens it to a particular page and reads, giving particular emphasis to words shown in bold.

'**Moreover**, if the merchants of any of these towns was robbed in Wales and the stolen goods not recovered in a week, the people could retaliate on any Welshman they could seize. **Even** in Wales itself, Welshmen could not hold **responsible** offices . . .

The room goes dim There's a flash of light, then darkness.

Teifion: On! Now!

She shines the torch onto the book. Teifion continues reading

Teifion: Welshmen could not acquire **land in** the boroughs, **nor** hold –

Boys: *(chanting)* RETURN TO SENDER, RETURN TO SENDER.

Darkness, followed by a large flash of lightning.
When the lights come back on, the desk is empty.

Kim: Where's the chair gone?

Zak: No one knows.

Kim: Are you telling me that's what happened to Fred?

They all nod

Dai: We put him there, to be our mascot. We didn't know he was going to disappear.

Zak: We always started the meeting with a reading. Nothin' never happened before.

Dai: Not till Phil brought that book in.

Phil: It's just an old history book. I found it in that cupboard.

Kim opens the book and reads from inside the cover.

Kim: RETURN TO SENDER. That's what you lot were saying, wasn't it? RETURN TO SENDER.

They look at her.

Kim: Don't you remember? Just before the lightning, you all chanted 'RETURN TO SENDER. RETURN TO SENDER'.

Teifion: We did?

Dai: It's the book. It makes you say things.

Kim: What sort of things?

Teifion: It makes you read a different way. When I read it, it makes me say some words loud and some words soft.

Kim: Rubbish!

Teifion: Alright, then. You try it. Tom, get another chair.

He hands her the book. Tom brings another chair and puts it on the desk.

Teifion: *(to Kim)* Read that bit.

He hands her the torch. She starts to read, and despite herself, emphasises the same words as he did.

'**Moreover**, if the merchants of any of these towns was robbed in Wales and the stolen goods not recovered in a week, the people could retaliate on any Welshman they could seize. **Even** in Wales itself, Welshmen could not hold **responsible** offices . . .

Once again the darkness and lightning come. Kim shines the torch and carries on reading, but her voice is trembling.

Welshmen could not acquire **land in** the boroughs, **nor** hold –

Boys: *(chanting)* RETURN TO SENDER, RETURN TO SENDER.

Darkness, followed by a large flash of lightning.
When the lights come back on, the desk is empty again.
Kim stares at the book, then comes to a sudden decision.

Kim: Tom, get another chair. Quick.

Phil: No. Don't do it. That's two chairs gone already.

She makes a face at him, gets a chair herself, puts it in position and starts chanting. But this time, all she says is:

Kim: 'Moreover, even, responsible, land, in, nor

Everything happens as before

Kim: (*excitedly*) That's it!

Teifion: What is?

Kim: Look at the first letters: there's M for moreover. Then there's an E for even. Then an R, then L, then I and then an N. What does that spell?

Teifion: MERLIN. It spells Merlin.

Kim: Yes. It spells Merlin, and it's Merlin's spell.

Teifion: Now it's your turn to talk rubbish.

Kim: It's not rubbish. Not at all. Don't you see? This isn't an old history book, it's a spell book. Look how the special words jump out at you. It only looks like a history book. It must be full of spells. That's why . . .

Teifion: That's why it has to be returned.

Kim: You got it.

Teifion: We were probably supposed to return the spellbook, not tortoises and chairs.

Phil: A spellbook. Here. Why?

Teifion looks at Kim and they get to the answer at the same time.

Kim: This school.

Teifion: Merlin must have lived here.

Phil: What?

Teifion: Think. What is this school called?

Phil: You know what it's called.

Dai: It's called Melin Arthur Primary. It means Arthur's Mill.

Zak: *(slowly)* Unless . . . maybe it wasn't '*melin*' in the old days. Maybe it was Merlin. Arthur's *Merlin*! Melin Arthur . . . Merlin . . . Arthur.

Teifion: I bet you, this school was built on the site of Merlin's house.

Dai: Wow!

Kim: And Phil stumbled on one of Merlin's spellbooks.

Phil: Let's send it back to him. Tom, put the book on the desk.

Kim: Not so fast . . . you can't give him his book until we get Fred back.

Teifion: And we don't know how to do that.

Tom: *(in a small voice)* Yes, we do.

Phil: *(pretending not to know it's Tom speaking)* Did you hear a voice? Who spoke just then?

Tom: Me. I did, Lord Rhys. I know how to get Fred back.

Phil: *(mocking)* How, oh wise one?

Tom: You got to say it backwards. Like this:

To everyone's surprise, including Tom's, his voice changes from squeaky to gruff and he recites in a hollow voice:

> NOR IN LAND RESPONSIBLE EVEN MOREOVER.
> RETURN TO SENDER WHAT IS OURS
> AND TAKE YOUR BOOK TO HELP YOUR
> POWERS.

Darkness.
In the flash of lightning that follows, we see, for a moment, the tall figure of a man in a cloak. Then another flash of lightning. When the room returns to normal, a tortoise is on the desk.

Kim: He's back. Fred's back. Thank you, Tom.

Teifion: How did you do that?

Tom: It just came to me

Teifion: Good for you.

Dai and Zak: Yes, good for you, Tom.

Phil: Where's the book gone? What's happened to my spell book?

They all look to Tom for an answer. He's pleased, but taken aback that they are all treating him so differently.

Tom: It's not yours, Phil. It's gone back to Merlin, of course.

In the silence that follows, Kimberly takes Fred back to his house and sees to him. Phil takes off his eyepatch and his hat and puts them back in his pocket, disconsolately. He feels most put out that the boys are now taking no notice of him.

Dai: What shall we do now, Tom?

Tom: Anyone want a quick game in the yard?

All except Phil nod. Teifion unlocks the door and as the curtain goes down, the boys follow Tom out of the classroom.

The Real Princess

(or Be Careful What You Wish For – You May Get It!)

Jenny Sullivan

Characters:
   Narrator:
      Mali:
     Melissa: } three girls aged about ten
      Rhian:
      Mam:
  Lord High Something-or-other:

SCENE 1: *Mali stands gazing into her bedroom mirror. She is ten years old, and is standing very straight. She wears a long nightie and a golden paper crown.*

The Narrator stands slightly upstage, facing the audience.

Narrator: This is Mali. Mali is a girl who lives with ordinary parents, in an ordinary house, in an ordinary street, in an ordinary Welsh village.

Mali: But I'm not ordinary.

Narrator: *(turning)* I didn't say you were. *(Faces audience again)* Mali's problem is that she really, really believes that she is a Princess –

Mali: I AM a Princess. So there.

Narrator: – who has these ordinary parents, ordinary house and ordinary life.

Mali: Quite by mistake. Anyway, who asked you to butt in? Go away, please. I'll tell them.

Narrator: *(hands outspread in question)* Tell them what?

Mali: Tell them that I'm really, honestly, certain that I'm a –

Narrator: A Princess. Yes, you said. But what proof have you got?

Mali: Well, there's this birthmark on my . . . on my . . . well, it's where I sit down. It's shaped like a little tiny crown, and everyone knows that's a sign of a real princess.

Narrator: *(sarcastically)* Oh, really? Well, I've got a birthmark shaped like a book on my knee. Does that make me a library?

Mali: Now you're being silly. Go away. I'm going to bed.

Mali gets into bed. The stage darkens except for a spotlight on the Narrator

Narrator: She really believes it's true, you know.

Mali: *(drowsily)* Because it is!

SCENE 2 *The school playground. Several children are playing ball, skipping, playing hopscotch etc. Mali sits alone in a corner. Rhian approaches.*

Rhian: Want a game of ball with us, Mal?

Mali: *(sighing)* No, thank you, Rhian. I'm sure it's a very nice ball, but it's only a netball, after all. It's not gold. *(She waves a dismissive hand at Rhian's standard netball)* That won't do at all. But, *(graciously)*, one thanks you for asking.

Rhian: *(crossly)* Blow you, then. Sit on your own and sulk. You and your silly stories.

Rhian runs away, bouncing the ball.

Mali: *(sadly)* No one understands. I'm so lonely. *(Sighs, stands up and says very dramatically)* Oh, I WISH my real parents would come and fetch me!

Thunderclap or roll of drums. Stage lights fade down. Spot up on

Narrator: Oh, that's torn it! Saying that just as the wind changed direction. Now you've done it. Everyone knows that wishing for something when the wind changes is the surest way of getting it. You'd think she'd know better, wouldn't you? Guess what happens next. Go on, have a guess!

Mali: *(off stage)* Get on with it, Narrator!

Narrator: All right. Keep your hair on.
I'll tell you. Mali had another bad day at school. Well, she would, wouldn't she? ALL school days are bad if you keep telling the teacher that Real Princesses don't need to do geography or sums and especially they don't have to do spelling tests. Anyway, she was ticked off about a dozen times, but when she got home, right outside her front door was parked this huge golden coach. All the neighbours were out on the street, or peeking nosily round their lace curtains. A very grand person stepped out of the coach and banged on the door. *(Rapping sound)*

SCENE 3 *A street of terrace houses. The very grand person is standing outside an open front door.*

Mam: *(wearing a huge wraparound pinnie, stands on the threshhold)* Oh, dear, look at all the neighbours staring. *(She bobs a curtsey)* Won't you come in, your Poshness? I've got a lovely bit of bara brith, and the kettle's just boiled. If you'll do me the honour, your Poshness?

Lord High Something-or-other:
> Tea? Good gracious, no! One doesn't drink tea!

Mam: How about a nice glass of pop, then? Mind, I've only got Lucozade pouches. They're our Mali's favourite.

LHS: *(snootily)* No time, no time. I am here on a mission. Their Majesties believe that, around the time of the joyful occasion of the Royal Princess's birth, an error occurred with labelling under the Royal Gooseberry Bush. Or else the stork couldn't read. As a result, you, *(he sneers, looking at the little house and Mam in her pinny)*, you received the Real Princess by mistake. Their Royal Ever-So-Highnesses got the, er, the other one. Complete error, of course. Both Clerk of the Gooseberry Bush and the Senior Stork have been severely punished. And as a result this, *(he gestures behind him)*, this belongs to you, I think.

Melissa creeps timidly on stage. She wears a long dress of shiny material, and a golden crown. She removes the crown and timidly hands it to the LHS, who takes it and puts it into a carrier bag.

LHS: Thank you, your Ex Highness. And where, may one ask, is Her Majestic Imperial Highness the Real Princess?

Mam: Our Mali? Well, here she is now, look, home from school. Wanting her tea, I expect. *(Mam gazes at Mali and Melissa, sadly.)* Well, well. There's a thing. Who'd have thought it? After all these years, too. *(She peers closely at Melissa.)* D'you know, though, I think he's right. You've definitely got Our Gran's eyes. Come and have a cwtch, my lovely.

Melissa, with an expression of delight, rushes to Mam for a cwtch. Mam looks sadly at Mali, who is standing beside the LHS with a huge smile on her face.

Mam: Shall I put Her Highness's spare nightie in a bag for her? And I bought her a new frock last week. I'll fetch it, shall I?

LHS: Good gracious, no! The Real Princess will have plenty of expensive royal things awaiting her at the Palace. *(Turns to Melissa)* Goodbye, girl. *(Turns to Mali, bowing deeply.)* Your Highness, your carriage awaits.

Mali waves regally to the goggling neighbours, lifts her short dress as if it were ankle length, puts her nose in the air and stalks offstage after the LHS. Mam looks after her, longingly.

Melissa: Are you really my Mam?

Mam: I suppose I must be. Come on, lovely, your tea's ready. *(She ushers Melissa into the house, but turns before closing the door, looking after Mali again, sighing)* I shall miss our Mali, for all her funny ways. I did my best for her, but she was always different from the rest of us. *(Mam dabs her eyes and closes the door).*

Narrator: *(appearing from the wings)* There! See what happens when someone goes and says 'I wish'? Always causes problems, doesn't it?

SCENE 3 *Darkness exept for spotlight on Narrator*

Narrator: So, off went Mali to the Palace, where she was welcomed by the King and Queen, her real parents.

Melissa settled down happily at No 14 Tudor Terrace. She was much more content there than she had been at the Palace, although it took weeks and weeks to stop her Mam curtsying to her all the time. But she'd never fitted in at the Palace. She didn't have a crown-shaped birthmark on her you-know-what, you see. Mali, now: that was a different matter!

Lights up. Mali is seated at a table, on which is a vast array of gold-sprayed plates, cutlery, glassware etc. Mali is sulking.

Mali: I'm fed up with posh food and I hate eating off gold plates. They make the butter taste funny and gold knives don't cut properly, either. They bend. And I don't want roasted peacock stuffed with candied swan for lunch. I HATE roast peacock. I COMMAND you to bring me baked beans on toast! With melted Caerphilly cheese on top! And tomato sauce! ON A CHINA PLATE! *(Mali's voice rises to a shriek)* NOW!

LHS: *(off)* Certainly not, your Highness. Real Princesses don't eat baked beans. And they never, ever, eat tomato sauce.

Narrator: And there were other problems, too. Some of the Palace staff, having never seen the crown birthmark, which was in a rather private place, weren't at all convinced that Mali was a Real Princess, and they kept putting peas under her mattress. Sometimes, she could hardly sleep for the pain.

Mali: And my bed is full of squashed peas. Fast as I scoop them out, back they come with another lot. Very messy. And green. And because I AM a Real Princess, of course, I can feel every single pea. I'm covered in bruises, look!

Narrator: And although the King and Queen were pleased to have their Real Princess safely home, once they'd dressed her up in posh frocks, and had her fitted for a crown, they sort of got used to her being around, and went on with their lives again, opening hospitals and motorways and going to other people's banquets. They forgot all about Mali. And Mali was used to . . .

Mali: *(miserably)* Lots of cuddles and cwtches. My other Mam and Dad didn't have much money, but they cwtched me a lot.

Narrator: And she had nothing to play with . . .

Mali: Except a boring golden ball. And that doesn't bounce properly.

Narrator: And no one to talk to . . .

Mali: Except that wretched frog. It keeps asking me to kiss it, for goodness sake! Who'd want to kiss a frog? Anyway, I'm not stupid. I know what happens when Real Princesses go kissing frogs. I'm much too young to settle down and raise tadpoles and . . .

Narrator: *(softly)* Live happily ever after?

Mali: *(miserably)* I wouldn't mind that part.

Narrator: *(turns to the audience)* So poor Mali had no one to talk to, no friends at all. She was sad,

Mali: And lonely.

Narrator: And miserable,

Mali: And ever so lonely,

Narrator: And dejected,

Mali: And ever so terribly lonely.

Narrator: You already said that. Well, you wanted your real parents to come and get you. You wished for it.

Mali: I know I did. But now I'd like . . . I want . . . I W –

Narrator: No! Don't say it!

Mali: *(louder)* I w –

Narrator: No! No! No!

Mali: *(very loudly indeed)* I WISH I COULD GO BACK HOME TO MY ORDINARY MAM

There is the noise of thunder/drum roll

Narrator: Oh, dear. Here we go again!

SCENE 4 *The street outside Mam's front door. Mam stands (still wearing her pinny) and Melissa peers over her shoulder at Mali, who stands outside, twisting her hands pleadingly.*

Mali: Oh, Mam, I'm sorry. I don't want to be a Real Princess any more. I want to be ordinary, and live with you and our Dad in our ordinary house in our

43

ordinary street in our ordinary village and be cuddled and cwtched.

Mam: Well, I must say I've missed you too, my lovely, quite a lot, really. Mind you, I like having our Mali around. But what will their Majesties say when they find out you've hopped it?

Mali: *(bitterly)* They probably won't even notice I've gone. Please, Mam. Can I come home? I'll try ever so hard to be ordinary, honestly I will. Please?

Melissa: *(quietly)* We could put an elastoplast over the little crown birthmark, Mam. No one would ever know it was there. And there's such a lot of love in this house, and tons of cuddles and cwtches. There'd be plenty for Mali, too. Please, Mam? I've always wanted a sister.

Mam frowns, thinks for a short while, smiles happily and hugs both girls. Arms round each other, they enter the house and the door closes behind them.

Narrator: Melissa was right. There were so many spare hugs and kisses and cwtches that the little house couldn't hold them all. Love came bubbling out of the chimney pot, and seeped under the doors and windows onto the pavement, so that everyone passing No 14 Tudor Terrace breathed it in, picked it up on their shoes where it stuck like happy chewing gum, and smiled all day because of it.

Of course, everyone in the Ordinary House, in the Ordinary Street, in the Ordinary Village in Ordinary

44

Wales lived happily ever after, and even the King and Queen, who were so busy that they didn't notice their Princess had gone, were reasonably content for Royal people. Eventually, they forgot that they had ever had a daughter. Everyone was happy, in fact, except the frog, who had no Princess to kiss. He thought he'd have to remain a bachelor for the rest of his life. And then he met a beautiful lady frog. But that's another story.

Yes, it all turned out happily. But don't ever forget. Take care what you wish for. One day, if the wind should change, you might get your wish . . .

The Ghost of Craig-y-Frân

Keith West

Characters:

Catrin Phillips: ⎫
Huw Phillips: ⎭ aged eleven and twelve years old.

Dad: (Dafydd Phillips)
Mum: (Mrs Phillips)

Daniel Morgan: ⎫
Kirstie Morgan: ⎭ Friends of Catrin and Huw.

Mr Price: Warden of the Outward Bound Centre at Craig-y-Frân Castle.

Ghost: a female phantom who doesn't speak.

Siân Pearce: kidnapped daughter of a rich business man.

SCENE 1 *It is evening and in front of Craig-y-Frân Castle there is a ghost, a middle-aged woman dressed in white evening dress. She beckons the audience with her outstretched hand. Mr Price appears on stage, the ghost screams and exits.*

SCENE 2 *The action changes to the kitchen at the Phillips house. Dad is drinking a cup of tea.*

Dad: Are you sure you both want to do this?

Catrin: Why not, Dad? It's great weather for camping. We don't get that many scorchers around here.

Huw: We can hire the hut out for just one night. The Warden will probably be pleased for some business.

Catrin: It will be good experience for us, Dad . . . staying at the outward bound centre.

Dad: You know there's been some funny goings on around this part of Pembrokeshire.

Mum: There's no need to frighten them, Dafydd. Really, you have no tact.

Huw: We do read the papers you know, Mum.

Catrin: It's all round the village as well.

Huw: That rich business man, Clement Pearce – his daughter has been kidnapped. Pearce has to cough up £100,000 or he will never see his daughter again.

Mum: Poor girl.

Huw: Poor girl? I bet she's a spoilt little rich girl. Don't think I'd rescue her even if I had the chance.

Dad: (*disapproving*) Huw! Anyway, we don't want anyone kidnapping you or Catrin . . . I haven't got the money.

Mum: You're heartless, Dafydd!

Catrin: Don't worry, Dad, the kidnapper will be miles away from here. If he's got any sense, he'll have taken her up the M4 to London. You can hide in a big city, but not around here.

Dad: I wouldn't be too sure.

Mum: Anyway dears, you'll be safe in the outward bound centre. Mr Price is a very nice man, I'm sure.

Dad: I'll take you both. I'll drop you off and go to watch the rugby. It's Swansea against Llanelli tonight.

Mum: (*teasing*) Grown men chasing a ball around!

Dad: It's the match of the season.

Mum: (*laughing*) Go on, off with you, boy.

SCENE 3 *Outside the outward bound centre*

Huw: They say there's a ghost here at Craig-y-Frân.

Catrin: Right, Dad, I'm coming to watch the rugby with you!

Dad: Don't be daft. Don't let Huw scare you.

Huw: I've kept this as a secret, but . . . Daniel and Kirstie are here too!

Catrin: What? They never said a word! That's brilliant.

Huw: We're going to have an amazing time here with those two!

Dad: Have fun, children. I'm sure the experience will be worthwhile. I'll collect you tomorrow teatime. Mum said, make sure you get plenty of fresh air. *(They all laugh. Then Mr Price strolls up. Behind him are Daniel and Kirstie.)*

Mr Price: Hello there. My name's Price and I'm the warden. I must say I'm not used to visitors . . . we haven't had any recently. Are you sure you want to stay?

Dad: No visitors?

Mr Price: They can't stand the outdoor life, see! Too many couch potatoes these days.

The friends greet each other while Mr Price and Dad talk.

Dad: *(to the children)* Be good now, won't you?

Huw: Yes, Dad. *(To his friends:)* Some hope!

Mr Price: I'm sure they will fit in with my ways, Mr, . . . er . . .

Dad: Phillips. I'm off to watch the rugby.

Mr Price: Watching, is it? We don't watch here, we do!

Dad: *(put out)* Yes, well, the kids like to do, that's why they're here.

Mr Price: Big rugby fan are you?

Dad: *(pleased)* A big Swansea fan, I am. They have a good team . . . the Alverston twins and young James looks good at the back. And that hooker, what's his name . . . Darlington . . .

Mr Price: Llanelli'll win, man.

Dad: I don't . . .

Mr Price: The game's a foregone conclusion, man. Enjoy the match, Mr Fipps.

Dad: My name's Phillips.

Mr Price: *(Ignoring Dad)* Right, first to the hut gets a prize. *(The four children run off to the hut)* Enjoy your rugby, Mr Fillets.

Dad: *(annoyed)* Phillips, my name's Phillips.

Mr Price: Ah, yes.

Dad: These were just fields when I was a boy.

Mr Price: I wouldn't know about that. I'm from the valleys. Didn't know the place until I came to run the outward bound centre.

Dad: These were the worst farming lands in Pembroke-shire.

Mr Price: Too close to the sea edge for farming, I expect.

Dad: I used to climb the castle, as a boy. Me and my mates. The trees were full of magpies. They used to come down and take off the ducklings from the pond over there. *(He points)* Not a nice place, Craig-y-Frân.

Mr Price: Why do you say that, man? Trying to frighten me?

Dad: *(laughs)* No, no. Then there were the crows. They took an extra delight in pecking out the sheep's eyes.

Mr Price: Oh.

Dad: I was glad to move from this place and into town!

Mr Price: I hope you don't go scaring your kids with this talk.

Dad: No, no. I've kept all this to myself. It's just now I'm back here. And all that talk about a ghost.

Mr Price: *(starts)* Ghost?

Dad: Didn't you know?

Mr Price: Don't believe in such things, man.

Dad: They said a man deceived his friends and they tried him and hanged him, in the olden days.

Mr Price: *(relaxes)* Oh, an old ghost, like.

Dad: Yes, what did you think I meant?

Mr Price: Nothing. Hey, you'll miss the rugby if you don't hurry.

Dad: Right. All the best.

Dad wanders off

Mr Price: Don't frighten me . . . nobody knows what I know. *(He looks towards the castle. The woman in white appears)* You don't frighten me either, Mererid. You don't frighten me one little bit. There is nothing you can do to me, Mererid. Nothing! *(The ghost disappears)* Now to see little rich girl. *(Exits)*

SCENE 4 *The castle dungeon.*

Siân: I'm hungry, Mr Price. If you don't feed me, you'll be in even more trouble when Daddy comes.

Mr Price: I'll feed you when your old man pays up. I'm still waiting for the ransom money. Cash, so I can leave this terrible place.

Siân: Just a little something, Mr Price. Anything, I'm so hungry.

Mr Price: *(relenting)* Well, you're no use to me dead, Siân Pearce. I'll find you some food. *(Exits)*

Siân: I hope somebody rescues me soon. What ever happened to knights in shining armour? Where are King Arthur's heroes now? I've read so many books, but in real life nobody rescues anybody. The only comfort I have is seeing the kind lady . . . but I'm only imagining her. She fades into nothing. She can't be real, can she?

Siân sits down and buries her head in her hands. The ghostly lady enters and looks on, sad and sympathetic.

SCENE 5 *At the door of the hut.*

Catrin: Mr Price, we've been waiting ages.

Daniel: I was first, Mr Price.

Mr Price: Well done, boy. Well done!

Daniel: What's the prize, then, Mr Price?

Mr Price: You can wash the pots, all the dirty dishes the last lot left behind, months ago.

The other children laugh.

Daniel: *(grumbling)* It's not fair. Some holiday this is !

The children enter the hut.

Catrin: This place is filthy. Look at all the cobwebs.

Kirstie: The smell is awful!

Daniel: We have a good view of the castle, though. If you look out of the window you can see the battlements. I wonder if this was built at the time of Henry Tudor.

Huw: Quiet, brain box . . . and get washing!

The girls laugh

Mr Price: Hope you're all settled in. You'll need an early night. Tomorrow I'll take you walking on the coastal path.

Catrin: But the activity sheet suggested we explored the castle, Mr Price.

Mr Price: *(looking shifty)* That's the old sheet now. Castle's out of bounds . . . strictly.

Huw: Why?

Mr Price: Unsafe, it is. The castle needs repairs.

Daniel: It looks fine to me.

Mr Price: The castle is unsafe. I'm locking you in now, just for a while. *(Walks outside and locks door)* You'll all get used to the place. Tidy up a bit, make yourselves useful.

Mr Price walks away.

Catrin: That's creepy, him locking us in here.

Daniel: I don't like that Mr Price. He was horrible to your dad as well. Rude.

Kirstie: We've done absolutely nothing yet, and the activity sheet promised us a time full of adventure.

Huw: Well, this is no fun.

Catrin: Perhaps we'll have plenty to do tomorrow. We just have to sleep in this smelly and dirty old hut tonight.

Huw: The girls' area is in the loft above. The boys' area is just off this room.

Kirstie: In the leaflet it said there would be loads of people here.

Daniel: But Mr Price said we were the first for ages.

Huw: I think we ought to explore this place properly. I don't like being locked in.

Daniel: People who lock others in usually have something to hide.

Catrin: It's like being in a prison! We paid for a holiday!

Daniel: Let's break out. There are windows.

Kirstie: I want to eat first. I'm hungry.

Catrin: Never mind that now – I don't like being kept like a prisoner. We're free, aren't we?

Daniel: It's nearly dusk already.

Huw: Mr Price had no right . . .

He is cut off by a scream from Kirstie

Huw: What's the matter?

Kirstie: There's a . . . ghost!

Daniel: Where?

Kirstie: Look out of the window . . . the castle!

Backstage, visible through the window, the ghostly woman walks across and out of view.

Huw: So, the ghost stories are true!

Daniel: She's vanishing!

Catrin: Yes . . . but she beckoned us.

Kirstie: This is scary.

Huw: Exciting!

Catrin: We must go to her. She might need our help.

Daniel: Well, I think we should stay in here. Mr Price must have locked us in here for our own protection. He couldn't actually tell us about the ghost . . . it's bad for business, but . . .

Huw: The ghost didn't scare me . . . she seemed sort of . . .

Catrin: Lonely.

Huw: Yes, lonely.

Catrin: We have to go to the castle, see if she's still there.

Kirstie: She may have been a . . . princess.

Catrin: She wasn't an old ghost . . . she looked modern.

Huw: A modern ghost?

Catrin: She was wearing an evening dress. She looked about Mum's age. Her hairstyle was like Mum's.

Daniel: I think we ought to stay here. Ghosts are dangerous.

Huw: Living people are more scary if you ask me. I've never heard of ghosts massacring people, have you?

Kirstie: The day's changed. There's a mist coming down.

Daniel: Funny, the forecast was for good weather.

Kirstie: Look, the white lady . . . she looks like she's on top of the mist!

Catrin: Like she's riding a horse.

Huw: She's looking directly at us, she's beckoning us.

Daniel: How does she know we're here?

Huw: We've got to go to her. She wants us to help her . . . like one of King Arthur's quests.

Catrin: Why did you say that?

Huw: What?

Catrin: The quest thing.

Huw: I don't know . . . I just said it.

Catrin: When you said it, I heard another voice, inside my head, a posh girl's voice. It said, 'At last'. Funny!

Huw: We must find out what the ghost-woman wants.

There is a sound of a rusty lock turning.

Daniel: Quick! Mr Price is here.

They all hide behind the door except Huw.

Mr Price: (*entering through the door*) What have we here?

Huw: Quick, run!

The others dash past Mr Price

Mr Price: No, you don't. (*He grabs Huw*)

Huw thumps Mr Price in the stomach

Mr Price: Ooof! (*He falls to the floor*)

Huw: Quick . . . the ghost is at the castle gate.

Catrin: (*off*) Let's follow her!

Daniel: (*off*) She's making for the dungeons.

SCENE 6 In the dungeons.

Kirstie: There's a disgusting smell of damp and mould down here.

Huw: The place is locked, but the ghost just walked through.

Mr Price: (*enters*) This place is out of bounds.

Catrin: Yes, but we saw a ghost.

Mr Price: Every castle has one! You shouldn't meddle with ghosts. (*Very firm*) Now back to the hut, at once.

Kirstie: Come on, let's go!

Mr Price: Now, what happened to the boy who thumped me? I want a word!

Huw has disappeared.

Mr Price: Back to the hut, I will lock you in first and then search for that boy.

The 3 children follow Mr Price. Huw emerges from the shadows.

Siân: *(voice)* Help me.

The voice comes from behind a locked door in the dungeon. Neither the audience nor Huw can see Siân.

Huw: I will if I can open the lock.

Siân: *(sighs)* At last, my true knight!

Huw: I'll get you out of here, don't worry.

Siân: I'm so hungry.

Huw: *(feels in his pocket)* I have half a chocolate bar.

Siân: Anything will do.

Huw: How can I pass the food to you?

Siân: There's a grill bar at the top of the door.

Huw: *(reaches up)* Here, take the chocolate.

Siân: Thank you . . . but hurry and rescue me.

Huw: I need to look for the key.

We see Huw searching back stage. In the front, enter Mr Price, with a key in his hands. Enter the ghost from the other side.

Mr Price: You don't scare me. *(The ghost comes nearer.)* Let me pass. You are only a phantom. You're dead. *(The ghost blocks his path)* I need to find the boy, before he finds that rich kid. Mererid, you always were in my way, woman! *(He is shaking. The ghost takes his key)* What are you doing, Mererid? You don't frighten me. *(At the back, Huw struggles with the door.)*

Huw: Mr Price is on his way. I can't find the key!

Siân: Hide! Or he'll lock you in here too!

Ghost appears with key in her hands.

Siân: The kind lady is here. I can feel her presence. I can't see her, but I know she's here.

Huw: She *is* here and she has just given me the key.

Siân: Quick, unlock the door.

Huw unlocks the door. Ghost exits.

Siân: *(Visible at last)* Where is the lady?

Huw: She vanished. Follow me . . . We must rescue my friends.

SCENE 7 *Inside the hut. The other 3 children are tied and gagged*

Siân: *(from outside)* The hut door is locked.

Huw: *(from outside)* It's not a strong door . . . we can knock it down.

The two push open the door.

Huw: Help me untie my friends, Siân.

Siân: We must be quick.

They untie the others

Daniel: *(To Siân)* Thanks, but who are you?

Siân: I'm Siân Pearce. Mr Price kidnapped me.

Huw: *(proud)* I've just rescued her!

Siân: There will be a reward. My father will be so relieved.

Catrin: But we have to find a telephone box.

Kirstie: Or an adult . . . or Mr Price will . . .

Mr Price: *(entering)* Now what have I here? Line up against the wall and nobody will be hurt. I am going to lock you all in and guard you from the outside. The ransom money is on its way. You are all too late . . . After tonight, all of you will go home. Nobody will get hurt.

Siân: But my father can't afford all the money you're asking.

Mr Price: Oh, he has found the cash, no trouble. He loves his little girl.

Mr Price laughs

Siân: You are a horrid, nasty kidnapper!

Daniel: Quiet, Siân. We don't want to anger him.

Catrin: Daniel's right.

Kirstie: You'll never get away with this, Mr Price.

Mr Price: I will. I have a 'plane ticket right here in my pocket.

Dad enters silently and he stands behind Mr Price

Dad: Not so fast, Mr Price.

Mr Price: *(spins round, shocked)* Thought you'd gone to the rugby man!

Dad: Now that's a strange thing! I wanted to go, but a lady's voice kept whispering in my head. She said, 'Your children are in danger', over and over. Now I remember Craig-y-Frân as a funny place. Thought I'd better miss the match. My children mean a lot to me, see.

Mr Price: You'll never hold me, man.

He pushes past Dad and off stage.

Dad: *(takes mobile 'phone from his pocket)* Don't worry, I contacted the Police as soon as I heard Price talk to you. *(He looks out of the doorway.)* He won't get far in this mist.

Mr Price: *(voice off)* Keep away, Mererid, keep away. Keep away! *(Screams)*

Dad: Looks like someone else is making sure he goes nowhere until the police arrive . . .

Siân: The white lady . . .

SCENE 8 *The Phillips Kitchen, two day later.*

Huw: It's in the papers . . . how I rescued Siân Pearce.

Catrin: And how Dad rescued you!

Dad: The ghost was Mererid Price, that poor bullied woman who was murdered by her husband. Well, she got some justice. He'll be locked up good and proper after this.

Huw: Dad, Siân's parents have invited us all to a weekend's boating around Skomer Island. Can we go? That'll make up for the outward bound trip.

Dad: Thought you'd like to go back to Craig-y-Frân Castle . . . there are other ghosts, you know, ones that go back hundreds of years.

Catrin:
Huw: } No thanks!

Playing the Game

Brian Smith

Characters:

Ioan:	Cadi:	
Richard:	Lisa:	Pupils in Year 6 at
Lewys:	Sally:	Derwen Primary School
Alun:	Meryl:	
Twm:	Kate:	

Mr Jeremiah, the caretaker:
Miss Moses, Headteacher:

SCENE 1 *In the playground, near the steps down to the boilerhouse. All the boys stand in a group; enter Mr Jeremiah*

Mr Jeremiah: Come on now, boys, away from here. You know Miss Moses has put the boilerhouse out of bounds. (*Under his breath:*) Interfering young madam . . . change, change and more change since she's been in charge.

Alun: We heard that, Mr J. That's the reason we've come.

Twm: We'd like a word with you, Mr J..

Alun: I was going to . . .

Twm: Say that? I know. I always know.

Alun: Just because you know what I'm going to say, you don't have to say it, do you?

Twm: Why not?

Ioan: Oh, cut it out, twins, we're here on serious business. (*After a deep breath:*) Mr Jeremiah, we'd like to have a man to man talk. Ask your advice.

Mr J: Man to man, is it?

Ioan: Aye.

Richard: That's it.

Alun: Man to man . . .

Twm: Like.

Mr J: O.K., boys. Fire away, I'm all yours.

Alun: It's about our new headmistress, Miss Moses.

Twm: Miss Bossyboots Gwendolyn Moses!

Mr J: Duw, steady on!

Ioan: It just isn't fair! Since Mr Hughes retired she's changed everything. It's just not the same any more. You're the only man left in the school and she bosses you around too.

Richard: (*High pitched and la-di-dah*) Don't do this, don't do that, don't go round the boilerhouse pestering Mr Jeremiah . . . he has work to do . . . blah, blah, blah, blah, blah.

Lewys: Don't climb the trees, no pretend fighting, no ball games near the windows . . . all in that posh, bossyboots voice of hers.

Mr J: Indeed, indeed. A new broom, boys, isn't it?

Richard: A new broom! I bet she rides it to school then. Did you know that the boys have to do sewing? (*Disgusted*) We're making cookery aprons!

Ioan: We thought you'd be in charge of the football team this season but Miss Moses has taken over and she didn't even invite you to watch the trials. She does seem to know the rules, though.

Richard: Yeah, but you can get that from books. What does she know about tactics and . . . and man management?

Alun: Nothing! She's only gone and picked a girl for the team.

Twm: The school football team!

Mr J: Bois bach! For the Derwen First XI? A female girl do you mean?

Ioan: Cadi Evans . . . Miss Moses has put her in midfield

Mr J: (*Spluttering*) Midfield . . .? A girl? Can she tackle? Can she pass? She can't have . . . she mustn't . . .

Richard: She has!

Ioan: Cadi's a good player, mind you.

Alun: But Lewys was reserve all last season and now Miss Moses has dropped him . . .

Twm: And put a girl in his position!

Ioan: So, we thought that as you used to help Mr Hughes with the coaching . . .

Alun: . . . and painting the white lines . . .

Twm: . . . and putting the nets up

Richard: . . . that you might help us to protest.

Mr J: Protest? Protest, is it? Aye, protest we shall then boys, until we get this decision reversed. A girl in the football team? It's a travesty, that's what it is, a travesty. It's . . . it's . . .

Twm: Unnatural?

Mr J: Exactly! First game of the season is next week. Graig Road Juniors if I'm not mistaken. We must act, boys. Act at once.

Ioan: We protest! That's what we'll say to Miss Moses.

BOYS (*Exit chanting*) WE PROTEST! WE PROTEST!

SCENE 2 In *the Year 6 classroom, just after morning breaktime.*

Kate: Well, I think it's great that Cadi's in the team.

Lisa: Not just in the team. Miss Moses will probably make her captain, mind.

Kate: Even better! She can make sure then that half the team are girls. Equal opportunities, and about time too if you ask me.

Sally: No one did. And anyway, eleven's an odd number. You can't have half and half. Not unless you divide two people right down the middle. Bit messy, that.

Kate: What are you wittering about, Sally? Aren't you pleased that Cadi's struck a blow for freedom? Boys have had it their own way for too long in this school. Three cheers for Miss Moses, Cadi and Girl Power! Hip, hip . . .

Girls: (*Except Sally*) HOORAY!

Kate: Hip, hip . . .

Girls: HOORAY!

Kate: Hip, hip . . .

Girls: HOORAY!

At this point the boys burst in and are joined by other boys in the class chanting WE PROTEST! WE PROTEST! Kate and the girls continue with their HIP, HIP HOORAYING and chaos threatens until Miss Moses enters and gradually makes herself heard.

Miss M: Enough . . . Stop this at once . . . Year Six, stop this . . .

Alun: WE PROTEST!

Miss M: NOW!!!

Twm: (*Whispering*) We protest.

Miss M: Sit down at once, all of you. Disgraceful behaviour, absolutely disgraceful. Really, some of you boys don't seem to have learnt any manners whatsoever.

Lewys: (*Low*) Bossyboots strikes again.

Miss M: What was that, Lewys?

Lewys: Nothing, Miss.

Meryl: Please, Miss Moses, he made a remark about you, Miss. He called you Bossyboots; he's always saying it. They all do. ALL the boys.

Alun: Tell-tale-tit, your tongue shall be slit . . .

Miss M: (*Warning*) Twm . . .

Alun: It's Alun, Miss.

Miss M: Sorry, Alun. I still get you confused. Now . . .

Twm: And all the little doggies shall have a little bit!

Miss M: Oh do be quiet, Alun!

Twm: Twm, Miss.

The class all laugh at this point and Miss Moses joins in, laughing at herself. Consequently the mood lightens.

Ioan: Alun's the one who speaks first for the twins, Miss.

Twm: And I'm the one who finishes off.

Cadi: Twm's the one Lisa always tries to sit next to, Miss.

Lisa: Ooo, Cadi Evans, I do not!

Cadi: You do!

Lisa: Not!

Cadi: Do, do, do!

Lisa: Not!

Cadi: Yes you dooooooo!

Lisa: Miss, tell her.

Miss M: That's enough, girls. Let's all act with a little more decorum shall we.

Richard: What's that, Miss . . . decorum?

Miss M: It means proper behaviour, good standards of conduct. Now, let's settle down and start our lesson. Take out your copies of . . . (*Sighs*) Yes, Richard?

Richard: Does it mean like manners, Miss?

Miss M: Sort of. Yes, I suppose it does.

Lewys: But according to you, Miss, only the boys have bad manners. It isn't fair. We always get the blame. Like when you came in just now. Everyone was shouting and you gave the boys a row.

Kate: It was your fault. You boys came marching in and you tried to drown out our cheers. And anyway, Mr Hughes used to be on your side. He called the girls 'giggly little chatterboxes'.

Sally: He always gave us higher marks, though. In our work and in exams and things. He did. Didn't he?

Meryl: That's 'cos we're neater.

Cadi: Take more care.

Lisa: We're much more attentive.

Meryl: Less messy.

Kate: Superior in every way.

Lisa: And prettier of course.

Miss M: Girls, girls. That's quite enough. This is appalling. I am shocked to the core. Do you really think I favour the girls over the boys?

Sally: Yes, Miss.

Kate: And quite right too.

Ioan: It's true, Miss Moses. Maybe it's because we're too chopsy.

Lewys: And mess about.

Richard: And don't listen.

Alun: Or perhaps it's because we can't sew.

Twm: Not very well, anyway. Not that we'd want to, mind.

Sally: Ioan can. He's the best sewer in the class.

Ioan: Shhh.

Sally: Well you are. You can sew and you can play football. And so can Cadi. And that's what all this is about, Miss Moses . . . you picking Cadi for the football team.

Miss M: I see. At least, I think I do. We're not going to get any work done until we've sorted this out, are we? I suggest that those of you who feel strongly about the matter come to see me during lunchtime. But I must warn you that as Head of Derwen Primary I am automatically manageress and chief coach of the First XI and I intend to remain so.

Lewys: (*Whispers*) Another bossyboots speech.

Ioan: (*Low*) Shut up, Lewys. Give her a chance.

Richard: Mr Jeremiah agrees with us, Miss. He says we must protest. It's a travesty, he says.

Miss M: Oh, does he now?

SCENE 3 *In the classroom at lunchtime. Enter all pupils, Miss Moses and Mr J.*

Miss M: I have invited Mr Jeremiah to join us as he seems to think an injustice has been done.

Richard: Hear, hear!

Mr J: (*Embarrassed*) Hummph, indeed.

Kate: CADI FOR CAP-TAIN, CADI FOR . . .

Miss M: That will do, Kate. We are here to discuss matters sensibly, not to play the fool. Now then, what are the objections to the team I have selected to play Graig Road Juniors in our first match? (*Silence*)

Miss M: Mr Jeremiah? I believe you have an objection?

Mr J: Well, it's girls, isn't it? Never had a girl in the first team in twenty-five years I've been here.

Kate: Sexist! Cadi can play, can't she, girls?

Lisa: She's good. Better than most of the boys.

Meryl: It's not fair if she doesn't get a chance. I'd like to play too. Mr Jeremiah doesn't know what she can do.

Alun: You play! You're hopeless! You'd fall over.

Twm: Trip over your tell-tale tongue.

Sally: Yes, I agree.

Cadi: Me too.

Miss M: Girls! Do be quiet. Have you seen Cadi in action, Mr Jeremiah?

Mr J: Er . . . no, not exactly.

Miss M: Well, let's ask the boys. Ioan?

Ioan: She's got a good left foot. Reasonable tackler, an intelligent player . . .

Richard: But she's taken Lewys's place, Miss! He waited all last season when we were in Year 5 and now he's not in the team.

Miss M: I thought selection should be on merit. Don't we want to put out our best team? Ioan, I intend to make you captain for the first match; what do you think?

Ioan: (*Slowly, truthfully*) Umm . . . it's a difficult decision, Miss. Lewys is better in defence and we're used to playing with him but I think Cadi is more creative and has probably got better skills.

Lewys: What!!!

Alun: Traitor!

Sally: Well said, Ioan. I think you're very brave.

Richard: Yuck!

Miss M: Hush! This is far too important for trivial squabbles. Don't you agree, Mr Jeremiah?

Mr J: Uhh? Oh, aye. Indeed.

Miss M: Right then, I have reached a decision. Lewys will start the match against Graig Road and we'll bring Cadi on at half-time. Is that fair?

Cadi: Yes, Miss.

Lewys: S'pose so.

Mr J: Aye, right enough. Then we can judge.

(*The children begin to drift off in ones and twos.*)

Richard: I don't know what's happened to Ioan. He's going soft if you ask me.

Lewys: Yeah. Did you notice that he's put flowers on his cookery apron?

Ioan: Sally, wait! Thanks for sticking up for me. (*Shyly*) This is for you.

Sally: Oh, Ioan, it's lovely. You've embroidered daisies on it. You can have mine when it's finished. I'm afraid it isn't very good. I've messed up the neck.

Ioan: That's O.K. I expect you'll be better at cookery than you are at sewing.

Sally: I hope so, but somehow I doubt it!

SCENE 4 *On the touchline*

Girls: COME ON YOU REDS . . . COME ON YOU REDS

Lisa: Come on, Derwen, tackle him . . . TACKLE!

Girls: G-R-O-A-N!

Kate: Two-nil to them! Roll on half-time, then we can get Cadi on. We need someone who can feed the ball through to our strikers.

Meryl: Who are they?

Cadi: The twins . . . Alun and Twm. We play with twin strikers, ha, ha. They've hardly seen the ball.

Lisa: Twm's playing well, bless him.

Sally: And Ioan.

Kate: You would say that, wouldn't you? Bimbos! There's no shape on any of them at the moment.

Cadi: How long to go?

Kate: Couple of minutes. Get warmed up, Cadi, and be prepared to knock 'em dead, girl!

Miss M: What do you think, Mr Jeremiah?

Mr J: Dire straits, Miss Moses. We need someone to take control of the midfield, stretch their defence and come through in support of our front runners.

Miss M: Agreed. An admirable summing up of our first half shortcomings. Do you think Cadi fits the bill?

(*The whistle blows for half-time*)

Mr J: I've been watching her in the playground. There's an educated left foot on her and she reads the game well . . . all things considered. In short, Miss Moses, she's our only hope.

Miss M: Excellent. Would you like to give the half-time talk?

Mr J: Me? Certainly. Indeed. (*To the players*) Right lads . . . and er . . . Cadi. Now then, listen . . .

77

(The second half)

Kate: ONE-TWO-THREE-FOUR, WHO ARE WE FOR?

Girls: D-E-R-W-E-N, DERWEN!

Miss M: We're playing much better this half, Mr Jeremiah.

Mr J: Cadi's made the difference. She's linking well with the forwards . . . (*Suddenly noticing*) Yes . . . YES . . . oh, good through ball, girl . . . classic play.

Girls: GOAL!

Kate: Nice pass, Cadi.

Lisa: Superb play, Twm! What a finish!

Sally: Ioan won the ball, he started it.

Miss M and Mr J: COME ON YOU REDS! COME ON YOU REDS!

Mr J: You seem to know your football, Gwen . . . Miss Moses.

Miss M: Call me Gwendolyn. Yes, my cousin Mel played for Wales.

Mr J: Not Mel Thomas, sweeper in the 1980's?

Miss M: I'm afraid not. Melanie Jenkins, fullback in the Welsh Ladies Team, 1996.

Mr J: Oh aye? Tidy. Now then, what's this?

Miss M: Alun tried to play a one-two with Twm but he was brought down.

Mr J: And now it's a free kick on the edge of their penalty area. COME ON YOU REDS!

Girls: COME ON YOU REDS!

Miss M: Come on, Cadi. Bend it round the wall.

Girls: YES! (*Cheers*)

Kate: It's in the net, it's number two! C'mon Lewys, give us a kiss to celebrate!

Lewys: Gerroff! What a shot! I wish I could do that.

Mr J: The equaliser! Well done, Cadi. A banana shot. Keeper didn't even smell it! I can't see us losing now, not with Cadi's midfield dominance. In fact, Gwendolyn, I think with this young lady in the team we're in for a good season.

Miss M: Indeed.

Mr J: Our next fixture is against Gors Primary. They usually mark man for man but if we play Cadi deep and use Ioan on the overlap . . .

Miss M: I beg your pardon, Mr Jeremiah!

Mr J: Oops, sorry. They mark person for person. But I reckon that with someone of Cadi's skill in the middle of the park and with Ioan's pace on the flank . . . (*Exit both, still discussing tactics.*)